YOUR KNOWLEDGE HAS VALUE

- We will publish your bachelor's and master's thesis, essays and papers

- Your own eBook and book - sold worldwide in all relevant shops

- Earn money with each sale

Upload your text at www.GRIN.com
and publish for free

Hardik Modi, Pragnesh Patel

3D Imaging: A Survey

GRIN Publishing

Bibliographic information published by the German National Library:

The German National Library lists this publication in the National Bibliography; detailed bibliographic data are available on the Internet at http://dnb.dnb.de .

This book is copyright material and must not be copied, reproduced, transferred, distributed, leased, licensed or publicly performed or used in any way except as specifically permitted in writing by the publishers, as allowed under the terms and conditions under which it was purchased or as strictly permitted by applicable copyright law. Any unauthorized distribution or use of this text may be a direct infringement of the author s and publisher s rights and those responsible may be liable in law accordingly.

Imprint:

Copyright © 2014 GRIN Verlag GmbH
Print and binding: Books on Demand GmbH, Norderstedt Germany
ISBN: 978-3-656-69700-8

This book at GRIN:

http://www.grin.com/en/e-book/276045/3d-imaging-a-survey

GRIN - Your knowledge has value

Since its foundation in 1998, GRIN has specialized in publishing academic texts by students, college teachers and other academics as e-book and printed book. The website www.grin.com is an ideal platform for presenting term papers, final papers, scientific essays, dissertations and specialist books.

Visit us on the internet:

http://www.grin.com/

http://www.facebook.com/grincom

http://www.twitter.com/grin_com

3D Imaging: A Survey

Pragnesh Patel
Charotar University of Science and
Technology. Changa-388421, Gujarat,
Gujarat,
India

Hardik Modi
Charotar University of Science and
Technology, Changa-388421,

India

Abstract —3D Imaging is a upcoming field with tremendous research opportunities and huge economical market. This paper present detailed information about birth of 3D Imaging to the present research. 3D Imaging has a huge market at entertainment level as well as at Industrial level especially in Medical Field. The contribution of various scientists for 3D Imaging is highlighted in this paper. Moreover present research work is also taken into consideration based on depth maps.

Index Terms—**Stereoscope, Brewster Stereoscope, Depth based 3D Imaging, 3D Photography, 3DTV.**

I. INTRODUCTION

Day-to-day activities of every person, whether it is driving a car in the street or playing a game of cricket, involve some type of three-dimensional motion tracking. Objects are seen in three-dimensional space and interacted within a varying degree of complexity.

For humans this is a simple task and is performed subconsciously, due to the astonishing nature of the brain. Reproducing this behavior in computers has been a constant challenge to the research community, with mixed successes and failures. Notable achievements include creating animated movies using the motion patterns of human actors, tracking the head movement of pilots in military helicopters and even creating robots capable of catching balls thrown at them. Most of this solutions are based on markers, magnetic techniques and mechanical body kits, and not on the more natural vision based techniques. [22]

The image systems such as photography, film and Televisions are trenchant systems. At present, researchers are making these systems more and more digitalized so as to make them capable to be handled on same platform of pixel based system. These pixel-based systems have increase in number of pixels and are also having rapid development. HDTV and UHDTV are examples of the same. Recent advances include Super high-definition TV which has about 100 times the

Pragnesh V Patel was student of Charotar University of Science and Technology, Changa, Petlad, Anand, Gujarat, India 388 421. He is now student of San Diego State University, 5500 Campanile Dr, San Diego, CA 92115, United State
Hardik Modi is Assistant Professor of Charotar University of Science and Technology, Changa, Petlad, Anand, Gujarat, India 388 421. He is pursuing Phd in Bio Medical Image Processing Field.

number of pixels of standard-definition TV. But is has a drawback of only one view. Future demands for more views at cost of even less pixels. This is a transformation of pixel based systems to ray based systems. Pixel-based systems had a single image as compared to ray-based systems with multi-view images. Rapid Progress due to intensive research work in light ray capturing have created huge market for 3DTV. Multi-View Imaging (MVI) will pioneer the ray based image Engineering. [1]

The roots of 3D Imaging were sown almost 170 years before in 1838 by English Scientist Sir Charles Wheatstone. He presented with stereoscope, a device used to view 3D images. Stereoscope is a device, which uses two photographs of the subject object captured from slightly different angles by two different cameras and when viewed together which ensures visual blending of two 2 dimensional images into single three dimensional image giving impression of depth and solidity.

The principle of stereoscope is as follow: Stereoscope requires 2 separate images that are taken from 2 cameras that are separated by a distance of few inches. User has difficulties in viewing when separate images are in absence of stereoscopic viewer. For two images to appear as three images, the user is forced to cross or diverge his or her eyes. Thus different images creates their effect on different eyes and thus user perceives effect of depth in the central image thus giving 3rd dimension to two 2 dimensional images. The images used in stereoscope are called as stereo cards.

A simple stereoscope has a tradeoff with the size of 2 dimensional images. However periscope like device becomes handy to solve this problem. They are called as more complex stereoscope using which user can see larger size images that have more information as compared to smaller ones.

It was in 1854 when world had seen first naval periscope built by Hippolyte Marie-Davy. It consisted of two small mirrors fixed at each end at 45° in a vertical tube. Simon Lake used periscopes in his submarines in 1902.[13] Sir Howard Grubb perfected the device in World War I. [13] A periscope is shown below which uses lens and prisms for focusing objects. Here a means mirror, b means prism and c is observer's eye.

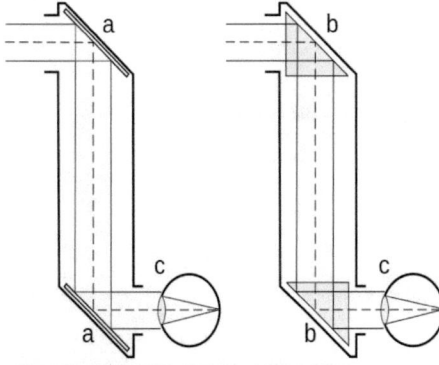

Figure 1 Simple Periscope [25]

Figure 2 Patriotic Stereo Cards [14]

A stereoscope for motion pictures has a mechanical setup described as follows. A drum that is vertically mounted with a wheel and a series of stereographic cards form a moving picture. The cards are controlled by a gate and on application of sufficient force the card bends and passes the gate. This brings the cards into view by obscuring the previous card. These force driven systems were coin-enabled devices which were found till the early 20th century. A hand crank was used to operate this system by viewer. [15]

II. HISTORY OF STEREOSCOPE

It was in 1838 when world first saw the first ever stereoscope made by an English scientist and inventor Sir Charles Wheatstone. He firmly believed that human eyes can perceive depth information i.e. 3rd dimension when two separate images of same object taken from different angles are given to left and right eye. The brain fuses the two images and a solid three-dimensional object is realized.

In 1839 the first practical photography process was invented and so in Wheatstone's stereoscope drawings were used. This stereoscope had the advantage of being size independent for images to be viewed.

David Brewster rival of Sir Charles Wheatstone credited the invention of stereoscope to Mr. Elliot. Mr. Elliot was Mathematics Teacher and according to David Brewster, the idea of stereoscope was presented by him in early 1823. It was in 1839, a year later to Wheatstone's invention of stereoscope; Mr. Elliot constructed a simple stereoscope without using lens and mirrors. Stereoscope was a wooden box with 18 inches * 7 inches * 4 inches dimension. Transparencies can be viewed easily as photography was yet to be invented in that year.

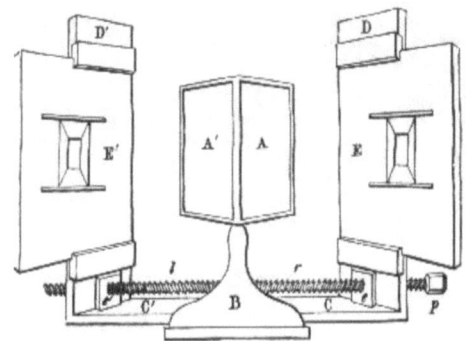

The Wheatstone stereoscope used angled mirrors (A) to reflect the stereoscopic drawings (E) toward the viewer's eyes.

Figure 3 Sir Charles Wheatstone Stereoscope [16]

It was in year 1849 when Sir David Brewster came into action and made a better version of stereoscope made by Mr. Elliot. David Brewster used lens for uniting the dissimilar pictures and thus lenticular stereoscope (lens based) was made. This reduced the size and creation of hand-held devices became possible. They were known as Brewster Stereoscopes which was much admired by Queen Victoria during the visit paid to Great Exhibition or World's Fair of London in 1851.The enthusiasm for three-dimensional photography shown by Queen Victoria soon made stereoscope a popular form of entertainment world-wide.

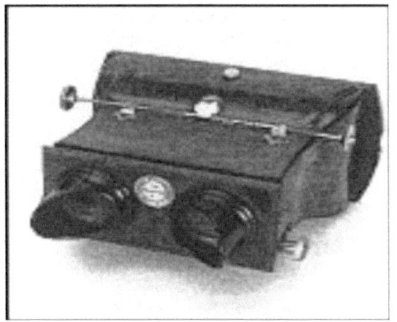

Figure 4 Brewster Stereoscope [17]

Brewster stereoscope introduced in London saw 250,000 units sold in a span of just 3 months. After huge success Brewster Stereoscope saw down fall in its demand as more power full stereoscope was introduced by Scientist Holmes in year 1861.

Oliver Wendell Holmes did not patent his invention. The stereoscope invented by him was much economical and easily handled handheld device. This stereoscope housed two prismatic lenses for giving effect of human eyes and a stand made from wood to hold the stereo card. Such economical and easily handled stereoscope was produce for more than a period of century. Holmes belonged to Mexico and hence it is often named as "Mexican stereoscope".

Figure 5 Holmes Stereoscope [24]

Almost after a century View-Master stereoscope was patented in 1939 that had rotating cardboard disks to place image pairs. In 2010, Hasbro started production of stereoscope designed with a holder to hold an iPhone or iPod Touch. It was named as My3D. Stereo-cards were provided by Application installed in mobile phones. This technology is unchanged from earlier stereoscopes. [18]

Figure 6 I phone MY3D app [23]

III. 3D VIEWERS

There are two types of 3D viewer technology, namely "active viewer system" and "passive viewer system". Active viewers house electronics which operates the display System. Passive viewers act as filters that block and pass constant and appropriate binocular input to the eye.

Active Viewer Systems

This system works by presenting the image intended for the left eye while blocking the right eye's view. The same is further repeated for the right eye. Repetition and Rapid changes overcome the interference and 3D image is presented to the user.

The glasses are made of liquid crystal layer that have property to become opaque on action of voltage and transparent on removal of excitation. A timing signal controls the glasses by allowing alternating darkening of one eye and then the other in synchronization with refresh rate of display. [19]

Passive Viewer Systems

1. Interference filter systems
In this technique specific wavelengths of red, green, and blue colour are used for the right eye, and different specific wavelengths of red, green, and blue colour for the left eye. Eyeglasses filter out the very specific wavelengths that allow the wearer to see a full colour 3D image. Interference filter systems are also named as spectral comb filtering system or wavelength multiplex visualization system or super-anaglyph system. Dolby 3D system uses this principle. [19]

2. Colour anaglyph systems
In Anaglyph 3D system, 3D effect is achieved by encoding images using filters of colours red and cyan. The image for each eye is encoded separately. When these separate images are presented to eyes through Colour Coded Anaglyph Glasses a stereoscopic image is formed. The visual cortex of the brain completes the further job of fusing the images into perception of 3D image. [19]

3. Polarization systems

Polarizing Filters or Displays equipped with polarizing filters are used in these systems. Display Systems are silver screen, so that polarization is preserved. Low cost eye glasses with opposite polarizing filters are needed. Viewers wear this glasses and polarizers block opposite polarized light and passes same polarized light. This makes it possible for showing different images to different eyes. [19]

IV. TIMELINE OF 3D PHOTOGRAPHY

3D photography has existed for over 170 years. In 1838 Professor Charles Wheatstone found out that human-beings perceive depth information on combination of two slightly different images. This capability of Human Brain was believed to allow us to see the world in three dimensions. To prove the proposed theory, Wheatstone made an instrument called the stereoscope to view images, known as stereographs.

At the same time, process of putting pictures on paper through the action of light i.e. Photography was invented by Mr. Fox Talbot. Next fifty years saw rapid development of photography and it became most popular tool of entertainment. It can be compared to Television these days. [20]

In 1851 David Brewster introduced stereoscope in London. 250000 pieces of stereoscope were sold in London in short span of 3 months. In 1860 Oliver Wendell Holmes introduced stereoscope in United States. 300000 units of this stereoscope were sold in 6 months. Meanwhile President Lincoln became the first President who was photographed in 3D.[20] The Kodak Brownie camera murdered stereo Photography in 1900 which was available for $1.

In 1922 first 3D film was developed named as "The Power of Love". It was the only film released in two – camera, two – projector stereoscopic (3-D) process developed by Harry K. Fairhall and Robert F. Elder. [20]

Interests in Colour 3D stereo Photography was regained back by View Master, Koda-chrome and the Realist Camera which reached its pinnacle during 1950. In 1935 Koda-chrome Colour Camera was introduced. In 1938 View Master and in 1946 Realist introduced Stereo Camera. [20]

Until 1974 Teapot became one of the most popular 3D object that was rendered for the first time. Interest in stereo photography declined rapidly after the introduction of Kodak Instamatic and Polarid Colour Cameras. [20]

Year	Event
1982	An episode of weekly science show "The Real World" was the first ever 3D broadcast in UK. The proper effect was possible to see only in red/green glasses.
1985	"Mercenary" became 1st video game rendered in real time 3D graphics was released.
1990	First version of 3D Max was released.
1992	Wolfenstein 3D was introduced to Gamers.
1995	First version of Blender was released for making 3D animations.
2009	Fujifilm Fine Pix real 3D W1was the first digital stereo Camera from major manufacturer.
2009	Avator film helps push 3D towards mainstream.

Table 1 - 3D imaging timeline for last 3 decades [21]

V. PRESENT WORK

Depth based generation of 3D images is under research and have gained success to certain extent. Research to generate stereoscopic views estimating depth information from a single input image is undertaken in Catania, Italy. Vanishing lines or points are extracted using a few heuristics to generate an approximated depth maps. [5]

Depth-Image-Based-Rendering(DIBR) is new and key technology in advanced three dimensional television system (3D TV System)[12][3]. Traditional 3D TV system requires the transmission of two video streams, the left and right view, to construct 3D vision. Unlike the traditional method, the advanced three dimensional television systems proposed a novel technology "DIBR" to provide 3D vision. DIBR uses intermediate view and intermediate depth map to render left and right view.

Multi-view image capture, 3-D scene representation, coding, transmission, rendering, and display are essential parts of 3DTV. It is very difficult to build a system captures and store a large number of videos in real time. An accurate calibration of camera position and color property is of more importance. Choosing of a 3D scene from the acquired multi-view data is equally important. 3-D scene is chosen in such a way that it becomes easy for latter processes. The amount of multi-view image data is usually huge, hence the data compressing and streaming with less degradation and delay over limited bandwidth are also challenging tasks. [7]

Various challenging tasks that include capturing and rendering processes and technical solutions are broadly reviewed in "Image-Based Rendering and Synthesis" [7]. The article, titled "Plenoptic Manifolds" [8] introduces a new 3-D representation. The compression process is broadly reviewed in, "Compressing Time-Varying Visual Content" [9] and "Multiview Compression" [10] provides a review of multiview video compression. The streaming process is addressed in the article "3DTV over IP" [11].

Figure 7 Original Image on right and unprocessed Depth Image on right [2]

Depth image is a 2D image that gives depth value to a point on an object in real scene according to its image coordinates [4]. Once intermediate image and depth image is given, any nearby image can be synthesized by mapping pixel coordinates one by one according to its depth value.

However, there is an essential problem in DIBR that occlusion holes appear after pixel to pixel mapping. Holes appear due to sharp horizontal changes in depth image, thus the location and size of holes differ from frame to frame. For hole-filling, average filter is commonly used [4]. However, the average filter does not preserve edge information of the interpolated area. [6]

VI. CONCLUSION

In this paper, we have studied the history of 3D Imaging or stereography. 3D Image Processing is the future in Television and other entertainment media. This field has huge opportunities for research oriented carrier. Medical Field is yet another field which will be greatly benefited by applications developed using 3D Image Processing.

VII. ACKNOWLEDGEMENTS

We would like to thank the Charotar University of Science and Technology for its support all the way through our work.

VIII. REFERENCES

[1] Zhang, Cha. "Multiview imaging and 3DTV." IEEE Signal Processing Magazine1053, no. 5888/07 (2007).

[2] Zhang, Liang, and Wa James Tam. "Stereoscopic image generation based on depth images for 3D TV." Broadcasting, IEEE Transactions on 51, no. 2 (2005): 191-199

[3] C. Fehn, K. Hopf and Q. Quante, "Key Technologies foran Advanced 3D-TV System " In Proceedings of SPIEThree-Dimensional TV, Video and Display III, Philadephia, PA, USA, October 2004.pp. 66-80.

[4] Chung J. Kuo, Ching Liao, and Ching C. Jin, "STEREOSCOPIC IMAGE GENERATION BASED ON DEPTH IMAGES", ICIP, Singapore, October. 2004, pp. 2993-2996

[5] Battiato, Sebastiano, Alessandro Capra, Salvatore Curti, and Marco La Cascia. "3D stereoscopic image pairs by depth-map generation." In 3D Data Processing, Visualization and Transmission, 2004. 3DPVT 2004. Proceedings. 2nd International Symposium on, pp. 124-131. IEEE, 2004.

[6] Chen, Wan-Yu, Yu-Lin Chang, Shyh-Feng Lin, Li-Fu Ding, and Liang-Gee Chen. "Efficient depth image based rendering with edge dependent depth filter and interpolation." In Multimedia and Expo, 2005. ICME 2005. IEEE International Conference on, pp. 1314-1317. IEEE, 2005.

[7] S.C. Chan, H.Y. Shum, and K.T. Ng, "Image-based rendering and synthesis," IEEE Signal Processing Mag. vol. 24, no. 7, pp. 22–33, Nov. 2007.

[8] J. Berent and P. Luigi Dragotti, "Plenoptic manifolds," IEEE Signal Processing. Mag., vol. 24, no. 7, pp. 34–44, Nov. 2007.

[9] K. Müller, P. Merkle, and T. Wiegand, "Compressing time-varying visual content," IEEE Signal Processing Mag., vol. 24, no. 7, pp. 58–67, Nov. 2007.

[10] M. Flierl and B. Girod, "Multiview video compression," IEEE Signal ProcessingMag., vol. 24, no. 7, pp. 66–76, Nov. 2007.

[11] A. Murat Tekalp, E. Kurutepe, and M. Reha Civanlar, "3DTV over IP," IEEE Signal Processing Mag., vol. 24, no. 7, pp. 77–87, Nov. 2007.

[12] A. Redert, M. Op de Beeck, C. Fehn, W. IJsselsteijn, M. Pollefeys, L. Van Gool, E. Ofek, I. Sexton, P. Surman, "ATTEST –advanced three-dimensional television system techniques", Proc. of 3DPVT' 02, Padova, Italy, Jun. 2002.pp. 313-319

[13] Periscope Information: http://inventors.about.com/library/inventors/blperiscope.htm

[14] Stereo Card Image taken from : http://www.thecatladyantiques.com/images/good_stuff/jun08/Patriotic2.jpg

[15] Principle of Stereoscope: http://en.wikipedia.org/wiki/Stereoscope

[16] Wheatstone Stereoscope Image taken from: http://www.bitwise.net/~ken-bill/stereo.htm

[17] Brewster Stereoscope image taken from: http://www.arts.rpi.edu/~ruiz/stereo_history/text/historystereog.html

[18] Information about Hasbro's My3D app : http://en.wikipedia.org/wiki/Stereoscope

[19] Passive Viewer System from: http://en.wikipedia.org/wiki/Stereoscopy

[20] Sam Ramadan's Blog about History of 3D Photography: http://blog.mission3-dgroup.com/2009/01/22/the-history-of-3d-photography/

[21] CGAreana for history of 3D Imaging: http://www.cgarena.com/newsworld/history-3d.php

[22] Abeysinghe, Sasakthi S., and Loganathan Krishanthan. "Three-Dimensional MOTION TRACKING USING Stereo Vision." (2004).

[23] Image of Hasbro Model from: http://www9.pcmag.com/media/images/298449-hasbro-my3d-viewer.jpg?thumb=y

[24] Image of stereoscope from: http://blogs.lib.unc.edu/ncm/wp-content/uploads/2013/10/Stereoscope_003.jpg

[25] Image of periscope: http://upload.wikimedia.org/wikipedia/commons/thumb/6/68/Periscope_simple.svg/220px-periscope_simple.svg.png